THINK IT OUT

HOW TO PLAN AHEAD

by Sloane Hughes

BEARPORT
PUBLISHING

Minneapolis, Minnesota

Library of Congress Cataloging-in-Publication Data

Names: Hughes, Sloane, author.
Title: Think it out : how to plan ahead / Sloane Hughes.
Description: Fusion Books. | Minneapolis, Minnesota : Bearport Publishing Company, 2022. | Series: Life works! | Includes index.
Identifiers: LCCN 2021039150 (print) | LCCN 2021039151 (ebook) | ISBN 9781636914282 (library binding) | ISBN 9781636914336 (paperback) | ISBN 9781636914381 (ebook)
Subjects: LCSH: Time management––Juvenile literature. | Children––Life skills guides.
Classification: LCC BF637.T5 H84 2022 (print) | LCC BF637.T5 (ebook) | DDC 640/.43––dc23
LC record available at https://lccn.loc.gov/2021039150
LC ebook record available at https://lccn.loc.gov/2021039151

For more information, write to Bearport Publishing, 5357 Penn Avenue South, Minneapolis, MN 55419. Printed in the United States of America.

CONTENTS

PLAN FOR IT!

There is so much to do every day. Sometimes, it can be hard to know how to get it all done. That's when we need to take a little time to think.

We need to get ready for the party.

4

Planning ahead means we can be ready for anything. Think it out!

5

A SMART START

A plan helps us work toward a **goal**. How can we be SMART with our goals? Try to be . . .

S is for **specific**

What *exactly* will you do?

M is for **measurable**

How will you know it's done?

A is for **achievable**

Is it something *you* can do?

Make a goal. Be sure to think about every S-M-A-R-T part.

R is for **realistic**
Is it too easy or too hard?

T is for **timely**
How long will it take?

BREAK IT DOWN

Some goals are big. They can be a lot of work. But reaching goals gets easier when we break them into smaller steps.

Planning steps helps us reach big goals.

9

STEP BY STEP

Checking off small steps is a fun way to finish something bigger.

TRY IT:

CHECK AS YOU GO

1. Think of ways you can break a goal into parts.

2. Write down the smaller steps.

3. Work on one small step at a time.

4. Check off the steps as you finish.

11

GET IT TOGETHER

How can we make sure we stay on track for our goals? By giving everything a time and place! A big part of planning is getting **organized**.

When everything has a place, we know where things are if we need them.

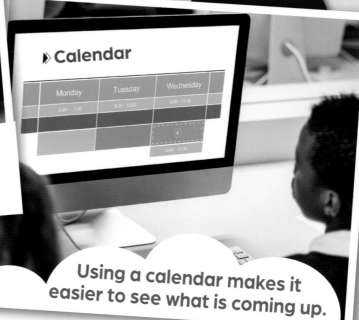

Using a calendar makes it easier to see what is coming up.

Make a **routine**. It's a plan
for the things we do every day.

13

START EARLY

Being organized can start before we even wake up. Try getting started for the school day the night before.

TRY IT:

WAKE UP READY

1. Pack your lunch.

2. Put everything in your backpack.

3. Pick out what you will wear the next day.

4. Go to sleep organized for when you wake!

Planning ahead the night before can keep the morning organized.

I'm ready to start tomorrow right!

READY FOR CHANGE

Sometimes, things don't go as planned. That's okay! It just means it's time to get **flexible**.

When we are flexible, we are ready to change things up. Being flexible can keep us on track for our goals.

MIX IT UP

There are many ways to reach a goal. Practice your flexibility to get from start to finish!

TRY IT:
MOVE YOUR WAY

2. Every three seconds, change the way you move.

3. Hop, roll, or move like your favorite monster. It's up to you!

1. Make your way from a start point to a finish point.

4. Keep mixing it up until you get to the finish.

19

THINK QUICK

It's easy to have a plan when we know something is coming. But what about surprises? It may be time for some quick thinking! That could take some flexibility.

Going through something once can help us have a plan for next time.

READY TO GO

Planning ahead gives us a way forward.
Like the dotted line on a treasure map,
it shows us where to go.

I know what to do.

Once we think it out, we can do almost anything. Plan on it!

Great plan!

Think it out!

GLOSSARY

achievable something that can be done through hard work

flexible able to change

goal something you are trying to do

organized planned or set out in a certain way

realistic able to be done rather than what is just hoped for

routine a regular way of doing things in a set order

specific clear and exact

INDEX